Children of BELIZE

THE WORLD'S CHILDREN

Children of BELIZE

written and photographed by

FRANK STAUB

Carolrhoda Books, Inc./Minneapolis

For Steve, my traveling buddy

Text and photographs copyright © 1997 by Frank Staub
Map on page 7 by John Erste © 1997 by Carolrhoda Books, Inc.

Carolrhoda Books, Inc. c/o The Lerner Publishing Group
241 First Avenue North, Minneapolis, MN 55401 U.S.A.

LIBRARY OF CONGRESS CATALOGING-IN-PUBLICATION DATA

Staub, Frank J.
    Children of Belize / written and photographed by Frank Staub.
      p.   cm. — (The world's children)
    Includes index.
    Summary: Describes life in the small Central American country of
Belize while following a variety of children in their daily activities.
    ISBN 1-57505-039-0
    1. Belize — Social life and customs — Juvenile literature.
2. Children — Belize — Social life and customs — Juvenile literature.
[1. Belize — Social life and customs.] I. Title. II. Series:
World's children (Minneapolis, Minn.)
F1443.8.S7 1997
972.82 — dc21   96-48981

Manufactured in the United States of America
1 2 3 4 5 6 – JR – 02 01 00 99 98 97

Boating and fishing are popular activities along Belize's Caribbean coast.

Tucked away on the southeastern coast of the Yucatán Peninsula in Central America lies the small country of Belize. The country's first inhabitants were the Maya Indians, who lived there as early as 2000 B.C. The Maya built great cities in Belize and much of Central America. Sometime around A.D. 900, most of the Maya in Belize moved to the northern Yucatán region in what is now Mexico.

Spanish explorers visited Belize in the 1500s. But the Spaniards built their main colonies in Mexico, Guatemala, and other places where they found gold. Spain claimed Belize but did not occupy the area.

Belizeans of many different ethnic groups work and play together.

British settlers arrived in Belize in the 1600s. They worked there mostly as pirates, raiding Spanish ships, and later became loggers. The Spaniards tried and failed to remove the British throughout the 1700s. In 1862 Britain officially made Belize one of its colonies and named it British Honduras. The name was changed to Belize in 1973 as a step toward independence. In 1981 Britain granted Belize its full independence.

About the size of New Hampshire, Belize has a population of 210,000. The country borders Mexico to the north, Guatemala to the west, and the Caribbean Sea to the east. About half of all Belizeans live along the Caribbean coast.

English is the official language of Belize. But on a bus ride from Corozal in the north to Punta Gorda in the south, you might hear Belizeans speaking half a dozen other tongues, including Spanish, Creole, Garifuna, German, and several Mayan languages.

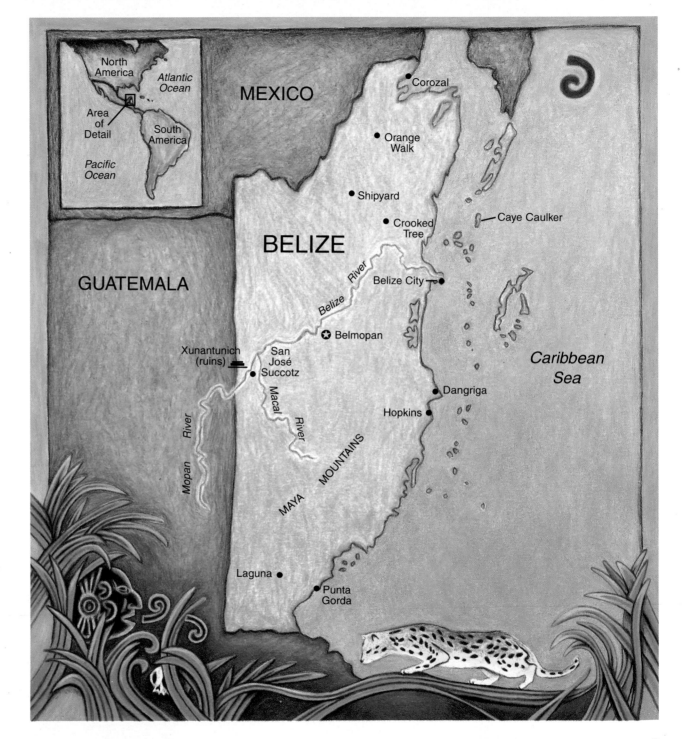

The toucan is Belize's national bird.

Deep in a rain forest in central Belize, a toucan calls from the treetops. In the bushes below, a tapir nibbles on a young tree. And down by the river, a big jaguar cat awakens to the laughter of boys and girls on a class trip. Their teacher has brought the children here to see one of the jungle's biggest trees. Belize lies in the tropics, so the weather is always hot and humid. In this moist tropical climate, the forests grow to be very dense.

The forests of Belize have played an important role in its history. Maya Indians cut down many of the big trees and made them into canoes.

The business of logging brought British settlers to Belize in the seventeenth century. They took slaves from Africa to Belize to cut down trees for sale in Europe. Despite the logging, Belize still has much of its original forest. Now the forests of Belize attract large numbers of tourists. They come to see the rich variety of plants and animals.

Students circle a huge tree to see how big it is.

The tapir, Belize's national animal, is a chubby forest creature with a long snout.

Jaguars can grow up to 7 feet long and weigh up to 350 pounds.

Eduardo uses binoculars to get a better view of birds in the forest. Behind him is a ferry that takes people across the river to the Mayan ruins of Xunantunich.

Fourteen-year-old Eduardo spends much of his time in the forests of western Belize. He works as a guide, showing tourists Belize's many beautiful plants and animals. Eduardo also takes visitors to see the ruins of the ancient city of Xunantunich, which was built by the Maya.

The ancient Mayan civilization thrived in this area from A.D. 150 to 900. The Maya made great advancements in astronomy, mathematics, and the making of calendars. They also created beautiful art, pottery, and architecture. Many of the stone structures built by the Maya still stand. One of the tallest structures in Belize is El Castillo in Xunantunich.

Daniel and Patricia live across the Mopan River from Xunantunich in the small town of San José Succotz. Like about 10 percent of Belizeans, they are Mayan. While their mother washes clothes in the river, Daniel and Patricia play in the water. Most of the Maya in modern Belize are descended from groups that came from Mexico and Guatemala in the 1800s.

Top: *El Castillo still stands 130 feet tall. The restoration of ancient Mayan ruins is taking place all over Belize and the rest of Central America.* Bottom: *Daniel and Patricia play along the Mopan River.*

Marvin waits for a fish to spear.

Marvin uses an old board to paddle his dugout canoe.

Just down the Mopan River, Marvin stands quietly in a dugout canoe. He watches the water for fish that he can spear. Years ago, when Central America had few roads, river travel in dugout canoes was one of the main ways people got around. Like the canoes of the ancient Maya, Marvin's canoe was made by hollowing out a big log. The ancient Maya made spear points from sharpened stones. Marvin and his friends make their spear points from the springs of old car seats.

Marvin also carries on the Mayan tradition of stone carving. He quit school early so he could devote all his time to his craft. He collects black slate rocks for his carvings from the bottom of a nearby river. A small carving takes him about a day. A big one takes three days. Marvin sells his work to the tourists who come to see Xunantunich.

Marvin with some of his stone carvings

Top: *Samuel and Yona dance to music played on traditional instruments made of mahogany wood. Emanuel Shux plays the harp.* Bottom: *Families in Laguna cook over open fires, use oil lamps for light, and carry all their water from wells.*

Samuel and Yona live in the small village of Laguna in the Maya Mountains of southern Belize. After the Spaniards conquered the Maya of Central America, much of traditional Mayan music was lost. But the people of Laguna are trying to bring it back. One man in Laguna, Emanuel Shux, remembers the old songs and dances. He enjoys teaching them to Samuel and Yona.

Elibiria, Concepciona, and Cleta enjoy learning the old ways too. But they also like to play modern games such as baseball. They don't have a baseball, so they use a soccer ball instead.

Each year, more and more tourists visit Laguna to see a traditional Mayan village. Some villagers make a living by providing visitors with meals and places to stay. Others make goods to sell to tourists.

Like most people in Laguna, Elibiria, Concepciona, and Cleta live in wooden houses with thatched roofs made from palm leaves. Inset: Four-year-old Liezama and her family live in Laguna. Her mother holds bracelets she made to sell, while her grandmother works on a basket.

Left: *T. J. rests after swimming in the warm water around the island of Caye Caulker.* Above: *Lorence (left) goes kayaking with a tourist.*

A long string of about two hundred small islands called the cayes dot the Caribbean Sea off Belize's coast. T. J. lives on the island of Caye Caulker. One of his ancestors was a British pirate who roamed the ocean waters around the cayes. During the early 1600s, pirates known as the Baymen hid in the calm bays behind the cayes and raided Spanish ships for gold and silver.

The cayes are sandy islands that do not support farming. Almost all food and other goods must be brought from the mainland by boat or plane.

T. J. spends much of his time swimming with a mask, flippers, and a snorkel in the warm water near his home. He likes to look at the many colorful fish and coral reefs. Just a mile off shore stands one of the longest coral reefs in the world.

Lorence is twelve years old and also lives on Caye Caulker. His father is a caretaker at a hotel. Hotels and restaurants are important businesses here. About one thousand people live on Caye Caulker, but thousands more visit the island each year. They come for its quiet sandy streets, friendly people, and clear blue water.

Miguel likes to collect bottles on Caye Caulker. He gives them to his grandfather, who turns them in for money. In another part of town, Joey and Jerry play soccer. Soccer is their favorite sport, as it is for most Central Americans. Caye Caulker has almost no cars, so the boys can kick the ball in the street.

Miguel, Joey, and Jerry belong to Belize's largest ethnic group. They are *mestizos,* which means they have Spanish and Mayan ancestors.

About 40 percent of Belize's population are *mestizos. Mestizos* first came to Belize from the Yucatán region of Mexico after a civil war broke out there during the mid-1800s. Thousands of *mestizos* and Maya fled into northern Belize and the cayes.

People still come to Belize to escape war. Brian's father came to Caye Caulker from El Salvador during a civil war in that Central American country. After school, Brian and his father kick a soccer ball on the beach.

To earn money, Miguel collects bottles in a sack.

Joey and Jerry (left) *and Brian* (opposite page) *love to play soccer.*

Early in the morning, on a dock in Caye Caulker, Morgan watches his father, Orlando, clean fish. Their ancestors are from Spain and Britain. Orlando usually makes his living by catching lobster. But the lobster season ended early this year because lobsters have become scarce. Orlando keeps only the big lobsters and throws back the small ones. He thinks that if all the lobster fishers did this, the lobster season wouldn't have to end early. Until next year's lobster season begins, Orlando will work as a fishing guide for tourists.

Town markets in Belize are great places to buy fish. Andreas Hacobo sells all kinds. He tries to sell as many fish as he can while they are still fresh.

Morgan watches his father, Orlando, clean fish.

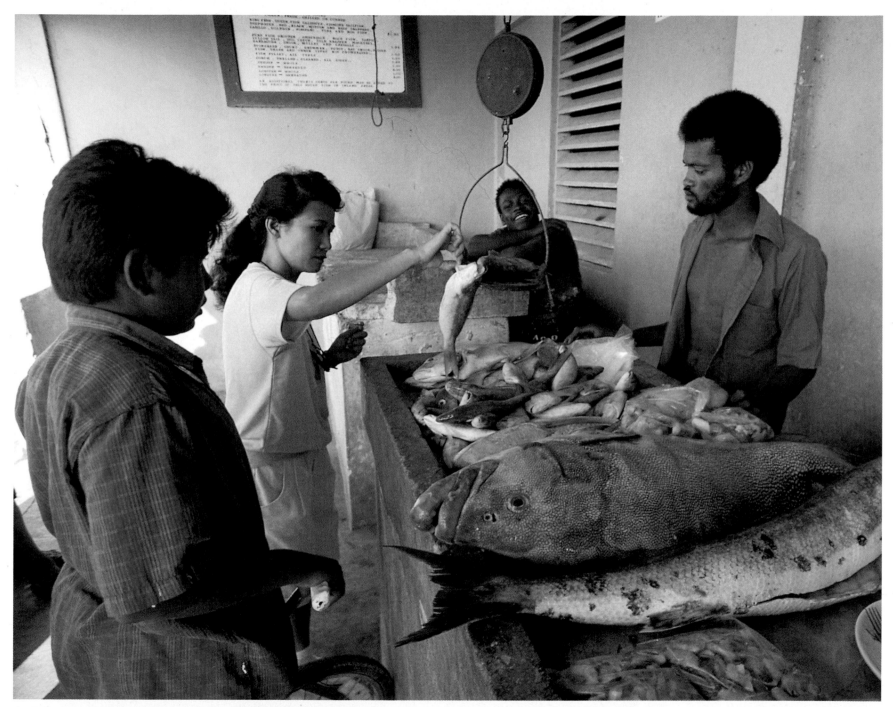

A customer at Andreas Hacobo's fish stand checks for freshness by looking to see if the fish's gills are still red.

Auria lives in the city of Corozal, at the northern tip of Belize, just south of the Mexican border. The city was founded by Mexican *mestizos* in 1849. Many people in Corozal speak Spanish, the language of Mexico.

Auria's father keeps his fishing boat at a town dock. Sometimes Auria sails out to sea with her father. They travel many miles from land in search of barracuda, snapper, jack, cowfish, and shark.

Auria on her father's fishing boat

Marcos throws his fishing net.

At another Corozal dock, Marcos and Fehrid catch the smaller fish that live close to shore. As Marcos throws the net across the water, he holds the end of a line. The line goes all the way around the net's outer edge. As the net sinks, he pulls the line tight so that the top of the net bunches together, causing the net to form a bag. Any fish inside the bag are trapped.

Fehrid shows off some of his catch.

Children in Belize are often expected to help their families earn a living. They also help with household tasks. Some catch fish, like Marcos and Fehrid.

Siyyid helps his family by taking a big box of buns and bread to the Corozal market. He carries the box on a three-wheeled cycle known as a carrycate. Siyyid's father bakes bread, and his brother comes to the market to sell it.

About once a week, Reymundo and his mother pull wagons to the forest at the edge of Corozal to gather sticks and logs for their stove. Many families in Belize have gas stoves, but Reymundo's family burns wood.

Frank helps his family too. He goes to the market to buy *masa,* a special flour. His mother uses *masa* to make *tamales*—a spicy dish of meat wrapped in dough.

Siyyid uses a carrycate to bring bread to the Corozal market.

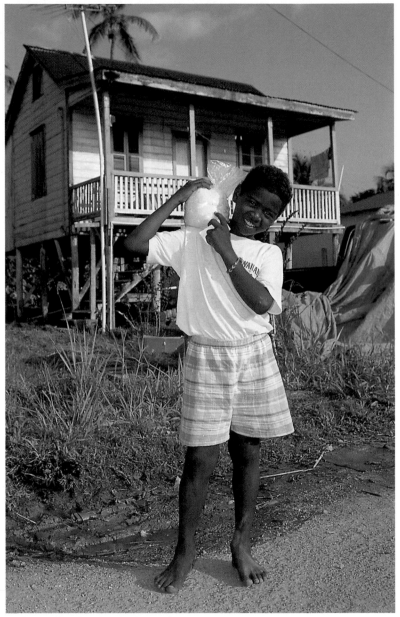

Frank with a bag of masa

Reymundo hauls firewood.

Trucks and tractors hauling sugarcane are a common sight in northern Belize.

About thirty miles south of Corozal, trucks haul sugarcane plants to the city of Orange Walk. At a mill there, huge steel rollers squeeze the sugary juice out of the cane.

Mexican *mestizo* farmers introduced the crop of sugarcane to Belize. Grown mostly in northern Belize, sugarcane has become the country's leading export to other countries. Belize also produces bananas, corn, grapefruit, oranges, seafood, coconuts, and lumber.

While sugarcane trucks roll down Orange Walk's main street, two young British soldiers named Robert and Paul load building materials onto an army truck. Although Belize is an independent nation, Britain has kept soldiers there to protect the country's borders.

Sugarcane plants in northern Belize

Spain had claimed Belize as part of its Guatemalan colony. When Guatemala won its independence in 1839, the Guatemalan government continued to claim parts of Belize. The people of Belize oppose Guatemala's claims, which are not recognized by the world community.

Robert and Paul load a British army truck.

George, Olbin, and Abner sit in the park before classes start at the Orange Walk Technical School. The boys study farming, machine repair, and construction.

In the town of Dangriga in southern Belize, Eden and Christopher finish up some homework before classes begin at the Epworth Methodist School. In nearby Punta Gorda, Edmar and John walk to a Catholic school. John wants to be a mathematician when he grows up. Edmar says he wants to be a scientist so he can "go to the moon and have adventures."

Belizean children are required to go to school until they are fourteen years old. Most schools are run by Christian churches, with funding from the government. About 70 percent of the people in Belize can read and write.

George, Olbin, and Abner in their school uniforms

Above: *Eden and Christopher outside the Epworth Methodist School.* Above right: *Edmar and John with two friends.* Right: *Outside the Catholic school in Orange Walk, students play and buy snacks before class.*

Urilla's house was built on stilts to keep it safe from floods.

Rasion and Akeem

South of Orange Walk, in the village of Crooked Tree, Urilla takes one of her family's horses for a walk after school. Urilla doesn't ride this horse because it likes to jump too much. She rides a more gentle horse called Old Nag. Horse racing is a popular sport in Crooked Tree and the rest of Belize. Urilla doesn't race, but some of her friends do.

Just down the road, Maryann and her brother George walk home from school. Like most people in Crooked Tree, they are Creole. Descended mostly from African and West Indian slaves, Creoles make up Belize's second largest ethnic group. About 30 percent of Belizeans are Creole.

Many people in Crooked Tree get water for bathing from wells dug into the ground. Rasion pours well water so his friend Akeem can wash his hands. People cannot drink the well water because it contains too many germs. So most people in Crooked Tree collect rainwater for drinking.

Maryann and George go barefoot, as do many of the people who live in Crooked Tree.

Marsha, Anna Marcy, Gina, and Romaldo also live in Crooked Tree. Their grandfather Donald Tillet is a descendant of British pirates called the Baymen. When Spain stopped shipping gold and silver in the mid-1600s, pirating was no longer profitable. So the Baymen became loggers.

The Baymen took many slaves from Africa to do the logging work. Work crews would cut down logwood and mahogany trees in the forest, then float the logs down rivers to the coast. The logwood brought high prices in Britain because of the colored dye taken from its wood.

Donald Tillet and his grandchildren

The children of Crooked Tree like to spot the many unusual animals in the forests, swamps, and lakes that surround the town. To protect these animals, the government established the Crooked Tree Wildlife Refuge in 1984. Before the animals were protected, Donald Tillet worked as a guide, helping foreign visitors hunt jaguars.

To protect the jaguar from extinction, Belize created the world's only jaguar reserve in 1986. More jaguars live in Belize than anyplace else in the world.

This trip to Crooked Tree is special for Lilyanna because Molly Tillet's dog just had puppies.

Molly Tillet, Donald's wife, runs a business called Molly's Cabins. She cooks meals and provides places to stay for visitors to the Crooked Tree Wildlife Refuge.

Lilyanna visits Crooked Tree with her father, Doug. He is a guide who gives people tours around the country. He often brings his clients to Molly's Cabins and takes Lilyanna along. Doug moved to Belize from the United States and married Lilyanna's mother, a *mestiza* woman. Lilyanna's grandmother is Mayan.

Lilyanna chats with Molly in the Creole language—a mixture of English, Spanish, and African languages. Lilyanna isn't Creole, but she speaks and understands some of the language.

As Doug and Lilyanna leave Crooked Tree, they pass a cricket match. Landis, who is at bat, plays on the Crooked Tree Brilliants, the same team that his father played on years ago. The British brought cricket to Belize, and it has been popular ever since.

Houses in Crooked Tree are surrounded by jungle.

Landis plays cricket with his friends every Saturday.

Cricket is played with a bat and a ball. It is very popular in Britain and in countries that were once British colonies.

Thirty-three miles south of Crooked Tree is Belize City, the largest city in Belize. The city is just a few feet above sea level, so it seems to pop up out of the sea. About fifty thousand people live there. Most residents of Belize City—about 70 percent—are Creole.

Every Sunday morning, Alicia crosses a bridge over a branch of the Belize River on her way to church in Belize City. About half of all Belizeans are Roman Catholic. Most of the rest belong to Protestant churches, with the Anglican Church being the most popular.

Saint John's Cathedral in Belize City shows the influence of British architecture in Belize. The cathedral was built by African slaves, with bricks brought to Belize from Britain. It is the oldest Anglican church in Central America.

Above: *Saint John's Cathedral was built between 1812 and 1826.* Opposite page: *Belize City.* Opposite page, inset: *Alicia on a bridge over Haulover Creek, a branch of the Belize River*

Steven and his sister at their father's stand

A Belize City street

Steven's father has a fruit and vegetable stand in a Belize City market. While his father works, Steven plays with his little sister. At one time, Belize bought most of its food from other countries. But by the 1950s, farming had replaced logging as Belize's most important source of income. Belize now sells sugar, fruit, and vegetables to other countries.

Some of the vegetables, poultry, and dairy products produced in Belize come from Mennonite farms. The Mennonites are German-speaking Protestants originally from the Swiss Alps. Large numbers of Mennonites moved to Belize from Mexico and Canada in the mid-twentieth century. They bought land and set up communities such as Shipyard.

Enrique waits for the bus.

Elizabeth and John

Enrique lives just outside Shipyard on his family's farm. On shopping days, he gets supplies in the city of Orange Walk and then takes the bus home.

Many of the Mennonites in Belize also make beautiful furniture. Every Saturday, Elizabeth and her younger brother John come to Belize City from Shipyard with members of their community. There they help sell hand-made desks, chests, cabinets, and tables.

Basketball is one of Belize's most popular sports.

Robert after a swim near the start of the Baron Bliss Cup sailboat race

Though they live in a city, young people in Belize City have many places to play. Robert and his friends like to play basketball in a park at the edge of Belize City. Later they will go swimming at the park's beach. Along the same beach, Veldimir plays with a boat he made from a broken coconut shell, some string, and a piece of glass.

Out on the sea, sailboats line up for the yearly race in honor of Baron Bliss. Baron Bliss was an Englishman who left Belize lots of money when he died in 1926. The money has helped pay for roads, schools, and other public projects.

Veldimir plays with a toy boat he made from a coconut shell.

Belize City used to be Belize's capital. But it was often hit by hurricanes. So in 1970 the government moved its headquarters fifty miles inland to the newly built capital city of Belmopan.

Maria works in Belmopan as a housekeeper for the Mexican ambassador. Each day she walks past the big government buildings on her way to work. The buildings were designed to look like modern versions of Mayan pyramids.

Maria and her little brother in Belmopan. The name Belmopan is a combination of Belize and Mopan, two of the country's important rivers.

Homes in Hopkins do not have running water. Venetia's family washes clothes in a tub of rainwater.

Six-year-old Venetia lives in the seaside village of Hopkins. She belongs to the ethnic group known as the Garifuna. In the 1700s, some of the African slaves in the Caribbean islands escaped. Many intermarried with Carib Indians who lived on the islands. The result was the people called the Garifuna. During the 1800s, some Garifuna sailed to southern Belize and started villages along the coast. They now make up about 6 percent of Belize's population.

Ela lives in Hopkins too. Her house is so close to the sea that it's almost in her front yard. She helps her mother by raking away some of the leaves and coconut shells that have washed up on the beach near her house.

Ela's neighbor, Denroy, cleans his grandfather's fishing boat before school. To scrub the boat, Denroy dips his brush in water, then dips it in the sand. This makes it easier to scratch off algae, tiny plants that collect on the boat.

Later that day, the sound of drums dances through the palm trees around Hopkins. It comes from Francis, who is practicing *punta* music. *Punta* developed from the traditional African music of the first Garifuna settlers. Drums are an important part of the lively *punta* rhythm.

Top: *Ela rakes the beach in front of her house.* Bottom left: *Denroy working on the beach.* Bottom right: *Francis plays a* punta *rhythm on his drums. People all over Belize love* punta, *whatever their ethnic heritage is.*

43

Several miles up the coast from Hopkins, people elected to the Dangriga city council are being sworn in. Elections are common in the democratic country of Belize. It has not experienced the revolutions and civil wars that many of its Central American neighbors have.

Political parties in Belize make billboards and give away presents to win votes. One party gave Emir and his brother Ivor a kite, even though they are too young to vote.

During Dangriga's swearing-in ceremony, Kwame Egemere reminds children that whether they are Garifuna or Creole, their African heritage is important. Each ethnic group in Belize is aware of its own special history. At the same time, Belize's healthy democracy makes it possible for the different groups to get along. Belizeans of all ages are proud to be part of their diverse country.

Belizeans vote at polling places, such as this one in Corozal.

A new member of the Dangriga city council is sworn in.

Kwame Egemere reminds three young friends that they must remember their African ancestors.

Emir and Ivor launch the kite they got from a Belizean political party.

Pronunciation Guide

Belize   buh-LEEZ
Belmopan   bell-moh-PAN
El Castillo   EL cah-STEE-yoh
caye   KEE
Caye Caulker   KEE KORK-er
Creole   KREE-ohl
Dangriga   dan-GREE-guh
Garifuna   gahr-IH-foo-nuh
jaguar   JA-gwahr
Laguna   lah-GOO-nah
Maya   MY-uh
Mennonite   MEH-nuh-nyt
mestizo   may-STEE-soh
San José Succotz   sahn-hoh-ZAY SUH-kutz
tamale   tah-MAH-lay
Yucatán   yoo-kuh-TAHN

Index